GW00786670

The Jellyfish Society

by

Lydia Popowich

e Jellyfish Society

st published in Great Britain in 2016 by Paper Swans Press
ems copyright © Lydia Popowich 2016
ection copyright © Paper Swans Press 2016

N 978-0-9931756-5-7

Foreword

When Paper Swans Press launched its first call for single-author pamphlets, we were looking to publish emerging poets whose poetry was both challenging and diverse. The poems in *The Jellyfish Society* span a range of subjects and are, essentially, about human survival. Just as jellyfish adapt and survive, so do we. In an ever-changing and ever-threatening world, these poems show us the resilience of the human race and demonstrate Popowich's ability to engage the reader through both subject and poetic form.

Sarah Miles

Editor

The poems in The Jellyfish Society defy pigeonholing. There is such variety here and such skill. Poems about the holocaust and ISIS brides sit side-by-side with a poem about a picnic at Wuthering Heights or a sinister take on In An English Country Garden. Strong poems, confident in every way. Startlingly good.

Carole Bromley

Popowich draws back the veil that cloaks transparent bodies of men, women and children - breathes life into their lungs and words to their throats. She deftly expose the haunting fragility of the everyday, the commonplace.

Abegail Morley

Lydia Popowich's 'The Jellyfish Society' is a pamphlet that pushes poetic boundaries delighting in the abstract and surreal. Not afraid to confront wide-ranging subject matter from Jihadist brides (Parliament has Consented to War) to a tender childhood relationship (Fry's Chocolate Cream), be ready for a colourful and astonishing read from this new voice.

Jill Munro

Here is the language of undercurrents, and 'small acts of sabotage'. In these hurtling poems we find a subversive, sentient lawnmower and ask questions such as 'did she ever find Heathcliff?' or end up in Hawaii? We are poised for a psychedelic meltdown in response to an dystopian collection that contains a 'dangerous box of stings'.

Jessica Mookherjee

Contents

Red Blush

Seized by the scent of sun on skin
I make the first cut, split the almost sphere.
The morning ritual slicing from the centre
around each segment, skirting the circumference,
parting flesh from flesh. Blood perfect,
topped with a glacé cherry
and served on blue china.

I want to cry out when she opens her gown
showing husks of missing breasts.
She was a stewardess before,
on the Queen Mary criss-crossing the Atlantic.
Now, she's the kind lady on Ward 5
sharing grapefruit with a braided child
as winter sun breaks.

Broken

I search
my home count
            -ry in fragments,
one cup smashed
            on cold, hard
tiles, the secret language of
            bone china.

Dinner
stories of
        striped pyjamas,
cattle trains,
        showers with
out water. Never forget
            twelve year old

boy hanged
for stealing
        boots from German
officer,
    Jewish girl
saved from drowning by Grandpa.
                He captured

her braids,
long black hair
       trailing lifelines
in rivers.
    War ends friend
-ship, fear hiding under floors
          like worms. Bombs

falling
silent be
    -fore death winds, spines
blasted out
     from their skulls.
Never forget Koyla's legs
       exploded

in air
raid, Allied
    liquidation
and Anna
    raped by drunks,
American marines, mad
     for power.

Never
forget Dad's
            horse weeping real
tears, left to
            starve. A lone
boy, guilt walked across the Alps
                        without maps

searching
for a home.
            Remains, one last
cup, perfect
            painted house,
trees, snow, hammer and sickle
                        underneath.

I drink
my coffee,
            admire the view
between sips.
            With careful
fingertips, I rinse clean my
                        home country.

Revolt

Like the Battleship Potemkin, rebellion
arose in the lower decks, dark
whisperings, small acts of sabotage,
a breakdown in the chain.
Then mutiny, paralysis
and the legs of war.

Like all revolutions, there was pain,
no longer running but stumbling
steps to emergency wards and scalpels.
Legless in a hundred waiting rooms,
the legs waited, abandoned by the ship.
They waited for orders, for rescue, for fate.
They plotted revenge and escape.

Like Tweedledum and Tweedledee,
the legs were not a pretty pair but easy to ignore.
Not the fashionable kind of rebels but survivors,
not stilettos but sensible shoes in a wide fitting,
not the soothing silk of stockings but skin
slashed by iron, rubbed raw by leather.
Battle scars saved
for the darkness of crumpled beds.

Fry's Chocolate Cream

The boy in the next bed was dying
of a disease with a fine French name.
No fruit, no flowers, no cards
wishing at his side. He had freckles,
curly hair the colour of coal tar soap
and Dr Barnardo's for a home.

We strayed, whenever nurses looked away,
used Fagin skills to pry Fry's Chocolate Cream
from the vending machine in Admissions.
The boy leaning on the push
handles of my wheelchair, dragging
numbed feet, sometimes losing a slipper.

At night the pain came stealing.
The boy, a brittle whisper
crept into my bed and I held him
close, close as skin,
nose to nose, forbidden
mint breath clinging.

Picnic at Wuthering Heights

Sundays, dad drives, mum folds
    maps, me in the back seat of our black Ford.
        We meander from Gargrave to Stump

        Cross to Oxenhope Moor. Stone-walled
    boundaries streak beyond misted glass. I choke
down nausea, cross fingers and legs.

Squatting in ragged robin roadsides, we search
    for traveller's joy. Weave delicate chains of wild
        amid the stench of exhaust. We chew hardboiled

        eggs, salamis, gherkins, hard cheese with red rind, wilted
    sarnies from Tupperware. Me and Mum sip tepid tea, plastic
brittle-edging my lips. Dad drinks Double Diamond.

The wind blows cold. We seek shelter in damp beneath
    dry stone walls ignoring the holes where carefully selected rocks
        fail to interlock. I look for Heathcliff in dark crevices, hidir

        secret notes, names scribbled on scraps. Northerly
    gusts breach the wall until we shiver. Whipped
silent, we scatter our crumbs and leave.

Sunday Service

Sum time is necessary to worship
shrine of hart, blud, bones, earth, sea, sky.
Stand eazee by the peephole in bright.

Soak stretch, smooth new leaf to wud.
Spread rein bows cross the empty feel. Use the rush,
softly sable, coarsely boar, flat fan, rigour of angels.

Spin the wonder wheel hot, cold.
Select sum taint quickly trickly, not too much.
Sway sum miracles this way, that.

Spare no sin, splot and splat, blot and blat,
slay the grey, stain the white. Copy cats
surrender. Scrap the map, snap the face,

state the world with graceful taint.
Sign your Marx on the whole,
sum time is necessary to show.

Scan the plan when ready and hang.
Shame nobody will see
sanctuary of yew.

Parliament has Consented to War

Shall I compare thee to a beheading?
My virgin thighs open wide in Jihad,
spilling scarlet in the dust of Raqqa.
Thine eyes shine hot with dreams of heaven.

For winter you need a good pair of boots.
Get all the vaccinations you require.
You will miss chocolate and Irn-Bru,
but a Kalashnikov is really cool,

you will need a small one for shopping trips.
Disposable nappies are hard to find
but no-one will abuse you in the street.
You can wear your burqa. You can be free.

Eleven thousand followers on Twitter
and I shall be watching you, my sister.

Note:-
At the time of writing about 200 young British women have travelled to Syria and Iraq to join ISIS in order to marry jihadist fighters and bear children for the Caliphate.

Desert Song

Put one foot in front,
    follow the other.

Why don't you
    keep your mouth

shut or sand will fill the empty
    vessel of your hour

-glass, counting down the spilt
    seconds to extinction? Never

peer through the sheer blind
    fold, Mother said was a necessary

precaution to prevent sunstroke.
    There's no place beyond

burning. Just listen
    to the hymns of the white

wind and the listless
    cries of children.

Tidal

The cruelest needs of the Jellyfish Society lie
deep in green pools of contagion. Each transparent
body, a branch, a hierarchy in the wasteland,
aesthetic as rain showering turquoise ink.
Citizens divided, pass uptown drunk with coffee,

pink sunlight sparking on the Burial Grounds of Scotland.
The physical marks grow like the tail of a crab

pinned to a donkey. This July she is a wedge of fear
but strictly not dead. Like most people, no heart, no brains,
no backbone, drifting in and out with the moon

trailing her dangerous
                    box of stings.

Apologies for the Turtle

I

If I write about you, will you go away?
Your reptilian stare, leathery grin, chilling
skin follow me everywhere. It's disconcerting.
You keep popping up without warning,
that alarming sneer, so hoity-toity!
Why don't you piss off back
down deep? No-one will miss
you here. You don't fit in.

Dump the rubber shell suit, try navy blue
anorak, polyester trousers from Tesco. Stop eating
strange fish. What's wrong with mince and tatties?
Your body odour is hard to ignore, try
Impulse Sweet Smile. Join the SWRI,
take up baking...I'm quite partial to a Gypsy
Cream. And I've been meaning to ask, why
are there jelly fish on your lawn?

II

I'm old as the sea and twice as deep.
I was born in the land where memories sleep.
History will keep repeating the subsonic beep
of your fears. Like surf drawing the beach
I will return, to be hanged by the neck
till almost dead but never quiet.

III

Being entirely ocean going, leatherbacks never encounter barriers in the sea
that they cannot swim around.

'They're not used to any kind of restraint, they've never seen a wall,' Jenny
McCloud, the aquarium's rescue director said to The Shetland Post.

'They'll continue to struggle, they'll continue to swim forward.'

Those We Miss

How many dainty flowers harden
in your English country garden?
Forget fritillaries and hollyhocks,
they'll rot away in the muck.
Bushy beard, broom sedge and swamp rose,
bull rush, cattail, marsh marigold,
bog bean, lizard's tail and bone-set,
panic grass, blue flag, turtle-head.
These all thrive on the edge.
Floating leaf mud plantain,
milkweed, smartweed, water mermaid,
duck potato are not afraid
of black eyed Susan and bittersweet
in your English country garden.

How many creatures ramble
in your English country garden?
Forget the sparrows and the wrens,
they'll not be back again.
Dragon fly, wood tick and mosquito,
crayfish, coypu, copepod, zooplankton,
snapping turtle, pond-skater and toad.
Sand-hill crane and great blue heron,
red winged blackbird, common egret,
these are birds you'll not forget.
No camomile lawns, in southern parts
caiman crocodiles with gaping yawns
and copperhead snakes entertain
in your English country garden.

How many toxic raindrops tumble
in your English country garden?
Forget the dancing in the rain
for you'll never be the same.
Boron, benzene, aluminium,
mercury, arsenic, titanium,
barium, formaldehyde, cyanide,
cadmium and many more beside.
Noughts and crosses played by planes
spray the skies with chemtrails,
vaping clouds. Weather engineering
taints your skin, heart, brain and breathing.
Blood rain, black rain, hard rains darken.
Forget English country garden.

Robo-Mow

Alan dreams 256 shades of green, hibernating
in his glass docking pod at the bottom of the garden.
Self-starting at sunrise, his solar panels slowly energise.
Recharged and updated with new kinds of seed,
66 brands of feed and non-toxic weed killers
plus the latest on invasive alien species.

Alan zips up his latex happy face
(with questioning eyebrows and a real pipe)
and his T-shirt declares 'I love life' (in bold font) for the Master.
After the BBC weather forecast, he initiates maintenance checks,
self-lubricates his cylinder, sharpens blades, tops up levels.
His friend, the virtual robin observes from a perch by the electric fence

Alan has the same old routine every day,
downloading music while he works
(Tom Jones, The Green Green Grass of Home on repeat).
Perfect, straight lines along the wire perimeter,
perfect stripes overlapping by a centimetre, working left to right,
raking, aerating, weeding, feeding as he goes,

forming perfect crisp edges around the lily pond.
Sometimes he hopes for showers so he can count
raindrops falling into the water, watch his reflection crumble,
ripple into concentric circles. Chaotic patterns
stir the surface calm, bubbles rise from the carp beneath,
flickering gold in the shadows.

The Midnight Caller

I see you waiting on the crocodile lawn,
the perfect blonde, my Lauren Bacall.

Your camel trench coat belted against the cold,
teeth knocking at my locked door.

To have and have not, a Lucky Strike.
Holy Mother how you smile!

I see you at the end.
Your skin is splitting face,

your hair is slipping free, skeletal
leaves in winter and there's nothing.

Remember

we gather at the edge
white feathers falling
in the dark
staring into the void
we are alone
the children wave purple lightsabers
kitted out in knitted hats
adorned with pom-poms
there's a sense of urgency
mother and child move quickly
the wrong direction
teenagers pace and stiffen into poses
words fade with the wind
the burning of wood
the Ivory Tower
the crackling of flames
taking hold the awe
exploding the shock
we gasp smoke
sparks rise shimmering bat-wings
it is beautiful
the stars weep green roses
silver snakes carved
in the perfect dark
a father thin and tired
carries his daughter
to the edge
holds tiny pink hands
in huge gloved fists
nuclear dots burn
in the emptiness
we hold the fire
and only the wind

Orbit

No-one noticed precisely when they began to vanish
one by one, without fanfare or farewell. Andromeda,
Cassiopeia, Hercules, King Cepheus, The Eagle, The Ram,
The Swan, The Whale, Orion and The Unicorn quietly fled.
No more wishes were left in the world but we pretended all was well.

Some blamed nuclear power, pollution, the depleting ozone layer.
Some blamed GM foods and the lack of home-grown carrots.
Some said the whole thing had been a lie, a false symbol of hope,
Christian propaganda, like the virgin birth and the three wise men.
They claimed the skies had always been an empty wasteland.

Some blamed a capitalist/militarist conspiracy, superpower
lasers and Chem Trails had dissolved every twinkle.
The Russians accused America. America accused everyone else.
As the nights hardened Daesh celebrated with mass decapitations.
Shrunken heads on poles made lanterns for the new caliphate.

At first we stopped going out, hid beyond the flicker of pixels.
But then Bot-Cops, plasma torches, quantum lights were invented.
The moon persevered in his solitary orbit. Children sang sky shanties,
hung fake stars from silk ribbons. Sales of glitter and luminous paint
rocketed. But then we all forgot, became too busy to look up.

When the moon began to shrivel like an old man's testicle
no-one noticed.

At Zero Hour

        sputniks gyrate
            inner space,
        strange **beep**
scares monsters in corners...
dance on, **beep**.
         Planning colonic torture, other shapes
           shift arm, hand as I write, sliding
             across, scratching like mice in the attic.
             The cupcake gist they are to whisk.
              Teeth gleam in sacrifice at hollow,
                crack fear from dawn eye sockets.
              The skull lets corners
                gather, the chances people **beep**.
                  My breath is percept, a.m. encircl
                Pandora is poised, holding
              one look-away thing.
              TV is a sin into other, the cast
             skin of silver aerials. The centre
            world is empty now, a snake
           gleam and glint.
        The empty skull **beeps** a double six.
Soon time to go, collect glass like left-overs.
Who is missing?
        Wires coil, my passport binding.
            The last three years of the future spirals.
           Our ship rotates
              space to un-destination,
               I hope its Hawaii.

Open Dark

A woman can make a million
when she downs the victory drug.

I would be typewriter with self.
I would be keys without doors.
I would be hands grown powerful.
I would be least still.
I would cross wild borders,
a wagon for home.
I dream of grass in crisis
and it is blue.
I am too late to quietly slip under,
too late to bring the machine.
I decline. I can,
maybe, wheedle a stick?
I am open dark.
I am heart of embers.
I am to have the man.

Time Travellers

Down separate years they travelled
to meet once more in this cold
spot, strangers now, another pit
stop along a gravelled road.
In this bog country, stars
cower in the grey blanket of night.
Before her, an old man, uncertain by the fire,
peat and pine logs still sparking
centre stage. Shuffling feet, hands stretched
out for comfort and heat. Hard lines; won
and lost this pretty gypsy boy, no longer choosing
time in the Tempest Café.

She's potent pink in the front row, sipping
gin fizz, icy as her fingertips. She drifts
across the borderline, remembering
wine breath slithering her skin,
the slip of red silk and the unzipping
of their youth. Oh, there was a time!
There was a time when paint flowed
unhindered across white.
Instrument against his thigh, he strokes the long, smooth
neck, notched like bone, a diminuendo encore. Strumming
her mouth, plucking her eyes, hammering her heart until
she slides, fret free, from her fucked-up life.

The Bag in the Bog

Early alarm, Tuesday, already. Sales meeting at nine-thirty. Me in dog house
probably. Power shower. Red or black, white or cream, toast or cereal?
Remember buy bread today. Clean teeth, empty dishwasher. Feed cat.
Defrost fish, clean shoes, forgot to floss. More tea. Leave note to milkman,
check e-mail. Turn on Radio 4; spies, lies, Cameron, austerity, food banks.
Obama bombs terror, sunshine, showers, intervals, fog in parts. Think positive.
Check bag; keys, iPhone, Mars Bar, Polos, Panadols, tampons, luminiser,
lipstick, mascara, tissues, iPad, pen, comb, compact mirror, sanitiser.
Stop for cash and petrol. Text boss. Idiot! Check hair, OK?
Lock door. Running late, play Taylor Swift, take short cut, Camster Cairns,
single track floating, peat bog, passing space, sleeping sheep, speeding car.

Archaeologists believe the 3,000 year old leather pouch discovered at Camster Bog
speaks the fate of a young queen from the Plastic Period who, through folly
misadventure, was deemed to have failed to please the Gods Apple, Mars
and Pan on whose benevolence her people depended. She made blood sacrifice.
The pouch contained phallic objects adorned with the names of her lovers;
Elizabeth Harden, Max Fatter and Christi Door suggesting that Plastics enjoyed
multiple partners in frenzied fertility rites. Androgyny was inevitable as male
potency and sperm count decreased. Simple signalling and recording devices
typically used by breeding queens to attract a mate were also found at the site.
Technos hope to retrieve images which may explain why Plastics self-destructed
releasing gender bender chemicals into the wild until the rivers ran red.

Some Like it Cold

In John O'Groats Marilyn is ready
for the fray, fresh lipstick, folded pink
napkins, polished counters.
And her namesake pouts from on high.

One scoop or two? She's ample
with vanilla, frivolous with fudge
frosting when the Orkney ferry men
drop by for cones and the latest crack.

The easterly ripples the canopy stripes,
keening like the piper from the pier,
the Pentland Strait froths whirlpools
of café au lait on the rocks.

End to Enders celebrate, guzzling
champagne, taking turns taking
photographs under the signpost.
By lunchtime Marilyn's low

on peaches and cream, high on rum
and raisin. She pops out for a fag,
sits on her bench in the car park reading
War And Peace as Stroma disappears into haar.

Herring gulls scout for wafers at her feet.
A bus full of Germans reverses past
the Edinburgh Woollen Mill, clockwork heads
turning her way. Mizzled tourists queue

but Marilyn is oblivious. The wind surges
and her skirts swirl like a snow flurry.
A sudden gust and she rises, bench and book
and all, up, up high into meandering skies.

Lydia Popowich

Lydia Popowich was born in West Yorkshire to parents of Ukrainian origin. At an early age she was encouraged to read Russian authors such as Tolstoy and Dostoevsky and began composing poetry and stories while still at primary school. Her maternal grandfather was a writer, photographer and political dissident in the former Soviet Union and he was one of Lydia's main influences.

After teacher training, a politics degree, various jobs and marriage she went on to study creative arts in Newcastle upon Tyne during the nineties where she specialized in photography and mixed media. For many years she worked as a community artist focused on health and disability issues. Her photographs and paintings were successfully exhibited across the UK. She was a Green Party activist, one of the founding members of Northern Disability Arts Forum and a campaigner for disability rights.

In 2005 Lydia moved to a remote coastal village in the Far North of Scotland where she lives alone with an Orcadian cat called Hope. Her poetry and short stories have been published in anthologies and magazines including the Dalesman, Northwords Now, Dream Catcher and Obsessed with Pipework. The Jellyfish Society is her first pamphlet of poetry.

Also published by Paper Swans Press

available from our online shop

The Chronicles of Eve is an anthology of poetry about women. The poems, from new and established writers, observe and explore the many facets of womanhood, what it really is to be a woman.

School is about learning: who we are, what we desire, how we interact. The lessons learned are not just those of Maths, History or Latin, but those of life. We are shaped by our teachers, our friends, our enemies.

Schooldays was shortlisted as 'Best Anthology' in The Saboteur Awards, 2016.

Romance is fleeting and what's left in its wake can be bitter, dark, destructive...

The Darker Side of Love explores relationships that are often hidden, but have a deep, penetrating effect on our lives.

Elisabeth Sennitt Clough's inaugural pamphlet, Glass, is filled with poems that are detail-rich, evocative and precise. Poems that invite us into their world of dark humour, transforming their readers and revealing their deepest truths.

Paper Swans Press is a small, independent publisher of poetry and flash fiction. We welcome submissions from all over the world and publish in a variety of formats: anthologies, individual pamphlets and online publications. Our aim is to give exposure and acclaim to excellent poetry and flash fiction. Please see our website for further information and current calls for submission: http://paperswans.co.uk